Sara Nesbitt Gibbons

And They Are Clapping

Indigo Dreams Publishing

First Edition: And They Are Clapping
First published in Great Britain in 2025 by:
Indigo Dreams Publishing
24, Forest Houses
Cookworthy Moor
Halwill
Beaworthy
Devon
EX21 5UU

www.indigodreamspublishing.com

Sara Nesbitt Gibbons has asserted her right under the Copyright, Designs and Patents Act 1988 to be identified as the author of this work.

© Sara Nesbitt Gibbons 2025

ISBN 978-1-912876-98-3

British Library Cataloguing in Publication Data. A CIP record for this book can be obtained from the British Library.

This book is sold subject to the condition that it shall not, by way of trade or otherwise, be lent, re-sold, hired out, or otherwise circulated without the author's and publisher's prior consent in any form of binding or cover other than that in which it is published and without a similar condition including this condition being imposed on the subsequent purchaser.

Designed and typeset in Palatino Linotype by Indigo Dreams.
Cover image by Neal Vaughan: nealvaughan.co.uk
©Neal Vaughan.
Printed and bound in Great Britain by 4edge Ltd.

Papers used by Indigo Dreams are recyclable products made from wood grown in sustainable forests following the guidance of the Forest Stewardship Council.

To the wolf, James,
and my beloved daughters, Corrina and Nico.
You are the heart of everything.

Acknowledgements

First publications: 'On Watching a Cob and Pen Kissing on the Serpentine at Sunset' was Sara Nesbitt Gibbons' first published poem, in Peter Ebsworth's *South Bank Poetry Magazine*; 'First', 'Escape' and 'Looking at her Missing Brother's Paintings: "Self Portrait as Child"' also first published in *South Bank Poetry Magazine*; 'Cinderella Explains Endometriosis and Subfertility' in *Magma*; 'Halfway Home' in The Emma Press *Anthology of the Sea*; 'Sign at the Start of the Road' in The Emma Press *Anthology of Slow Things*; 'The Intense Synaesthesia of Belonging' in *Bedford Square 6 (Ward Wood)*; 'First Sight of Real Seals' in *Porridge*; 'I will propose on Halloween' in *14*; 'Under' in *Interpreter's House*; 'To Sorrow' and 'Lines' in *Obsessed with Pipework*; 'Safety at Sea' in *The Lampeter Review*; 'Loss' in *Brittle Star*.

'Kensington Central Library (Red)' was commended in the *Troubadour International Poetry Prize*; 'Afterlife' was commended in the *Hippocrates Prize for Poetry and Medicine*; 'Looking at Her Missing Brother's Paintings: "East Finchley Cemetery"' was highly commended in *Frosted Fire's* single poem contest; 'Reading the Sea' was commended in the *Ware Poets Prize*; 'Green / Brown' was highly commended in *PenFro Green Poems*.

My endless thanks to: my First Readers, James, Corrina and Nico, and my Mum; my fabulous creative writing students in South London; Lucien and all that is Claremont; Peter Ebsworth; Karin and Micha; my Stanza group; Em, for the Glow; Colin Barnes, for the sea; Neal Vaughan for the Art – wow! and wow again!; Dawn and Ronnie for making the collection a reality; and, from the tips of my toes, all my lovely friends for your years of love, support and encouragement. Thank you.

And They Are Clapping is Sara Nesbitt Gibbons' debut collection.

CONTENTS

My Mouth Will Release Me 9

Green / Brown 10

Sign at the Start of the Road 11

Kensington Central Library (Red) 12

Word Wise 13

Looking at Her Missing Brother's Paintings: 'Mount Goatfell, Isle of Arran' 14

The Wait (Tajweed) 15

Cinderella Explains Endometriosis and Subfertility 16

Escape 17

Morrison's Box, first lockdown (after no food shopping for three weeks) 18

Tracing Home in the Old Country 20

Sky Blue Pink 21

First Sight of Real Seals 22

Wreck, Basement Flat, W11 23

Afterlife 24

University Dental Hospital, Tower Wing 25

Looking at Her Missing Brother's Paintings: 'Self Portrait as Child' 29

I will propose on Halloween 30

Shared Grief and the Orange of a Streetlamp 31

Under	32
Sleep	33
To Sorrow	34
Looking at Her Missing Brother's Paintings: 'East Finchley Cemetery'	35
Komodo Dragon	36
My Garden Explains Endometriosis and Laparoscopy	37
Halfway Home	38
Army of Teeth	39
Lines	40
Loss	41
Safety at Sea	42
Does it Snow at Sea?	43
On Watching a Cob and Pen Kissing on the Serpentine at Sunset	44
First	45
The Intense Synaesthesia of Belonging	46
Reading the Sea	48

And They Are Clapping

My Mouth Will Release Me

A piece still on the roof of my mouth,
these dry spelt biscuits take too long.

The grown ups around the dining table
tell me hush, keep chewing

and I do, I chew, I try, till I
am miles away, outdoors, somewhere sun

makes dust of the path, flakes of the walls.
The walls crumble where I climb.

Waves drag back the gravel.
The coarse piece will not dissolve, glued

stuck to the roof of my mouth.
Crabs scuttle to tiny rockpools.

Barnacles barnacle. Rain falls.
I jump. The air's a push. Rain

dissolves on my skin. My tongue
seals. At last the biscuit gives

with the rain, the rockpools, the tide,
and I land, as a wet glob of spelt,

like a splat of sand, goes down my
throat. My knees hurt. My feet are shocked.

There are other children and they are clapping.
There is a rainbow beyond the shingle.

The salt and pepper pots shake approval.
My mother nods, but I am already free.

Green / Brown

Let me explain:
a man arrived
to cut back the ash
and kept on cutting.

Every day I heard snippers.
I asked him to stop
but he wouldn't.
He smiled

and kept on cutting.
A clearing appeared,
large enough to play in.
I asked him to stop.

He kept on cutting.
He cut all the way
to the boundary
then looked back smiling.

Everyone leaned on
the broken fence
and stared
at the brown field.

It's no-one's.
I open a bottle.
Snip packets of seeds.
Come. Dig in.

Sign at the Start of the Road

I am thinking of my new lover
when it arrests me: a pole, in brambles.
Rust lumped into barnacle shapes
on its blue and white hoops. A mirror,
for cars turning from the beach.
Wholesale orange juice cartons, Lucozade.
Rusty ferns. Rust winter light.
My parents' dog disappears. They are less
loyal than they're cracked up to be.
A cloud makes a full, solid sheep. Now *that*
is how my loving feels. I look
at the barnacled pole again. I look and look.
What is it telling me about desire?

The dog is at the foot of the path, nearby.
He is waiting for me. I fake a leap.
He doesn't budge; stays strong and waiting.
I am not here to be put off by revelations
that my lover is like a rusty pole.
I'm here to learn about dogs. I near the dog.
He turns and heads uphill, I follow.
I come to realise my new straightness
and slowness. This is how
my lover walks. Upright and heavy-based,
outward as a mirror,
patient as rust or a barnacle.

Kensington Central Library (Red)

There are two rugs, one worn, one new. Each emblazoned:
Get Carried Away By a Book. I read here. I decode 30 years.
Mahogany fort with index, stamps and fines, gone. Here's
a kind lanyard at a help screen. CD section now tiny.
Here's where a man broke silence with an apple
and I made myself invisible on the window seat, looking
over the Great Piratical Rumbustification to Sticky Fingers.
We lost it all again and again and again, Kensington.

Here's the window seat, exposed now the shelf
and Hiawatha's gone. Still concrete breeze blocks.
Still the great, brass gates. They've always been locked.
My eldest on a cushion in the window seat, reading.
My youngest says, "Choose a different favourite," tugs
me onto the new rug, its same words. *Get carried away.*

Word Wise
Source: Kindle dictionary software definition errors, 6/7/20

Sure – clothing worn on one's foot
The – sound of a foot when placed
Rubber – to walk slowly

Stroke – a person you love very much
All – a small cup used to drink tea
To – a thick bed covering

Live – to hold closely with the arms
Love – ice or rocks that slide past
Open – not being able to think clearly

Up – located on the lower floor
Pink – to push with
Right – having the quality of a girl

Scrubbing – one who plans death ceremonies
Out – to laugh
Of – a hidden problem

Girl – items that are no longer useful
She – to rub hard with rough objects
Her – a strong push

Do – be or become upset or worried
Breath – a box used for a dead body
Be – breathe in suddenly and loudly

You – to become red in the face
Is – a strong feeling of anger
Again – a strong, flexible substance

Looking at Her Missing Brother's Paintings: 'Mount Goatfell, Isle of Arran'

You've painted either a path or a deep crack, with rocks, tumbling.
I feel nothing. I feel detached as any bit of dust around rocks.

I lick the dried mud on this new path made by tumbling.

It tastes like a mouth full of dried out words,
sticks on the tongue, around the gums.

Chokes me, a threat
of inward collapse,
the final revealing of a way

of tumbling rocks. A divide, a growing split
with all the appearances of a path

a return, a return to me.

The Wait (Tajweed)

Friends or neighbours, man to woman on the seat behind
giggles, *Noone tells you the greatest gift of your life
is also the hardest.* Like me they leave the bus for the hospital.

I try to switch off in A&E, flick my eyes to the wavering TV
where the band Little Mix celebrate the title that births them,
talent show winners. The overvoiced rage on Jeremy Kyle

turns me to a book I've been beginning for a decade: Chatwin's
'Songlines' – healing sight, staring at horizons, singing the world
into existence, the Uncle who recited surahs from the Qu'ran

and the Surah al Alaq pricks my tongue, the surah of blood,
the pen God took to write man into being from that clot.
The only surah I know. I keen for words to keep my child inside,

settle for reading till porter Len wheels my too-early bleeding
to the Labour Ward. Len wobbles the chair past bums of clerks
fettling a file-trolley, to the lift by a pipe room he says is roach-

ridden. He leaves me to wait for the midwives. Patient in silence,
I hear a woman roaring as she births, the cries of crows or
babies, feel my bleeding sealed by the message they recite:
                                                            grow to sound life.

Cinderella Explains Endometriosis and Subfertility

Sit, feet in water, on the edge of the bath,
light bulb bare as the cold light your deepest
cells dreamed, hot as diathermy on your neck.

Look at the glass urine pot you're smashing
into the base of the bath, so it's no longer
yet another proof you can't conceive.

Your wincing toes glance the hundred broken
slippers of your losses – the babies
who can't find their way to your womb,

or basement flat, where you must sit,
feet pressed with glass, calves in water
cut with light like a calming sea,

watch your legs fragment. Your body is in bits.
Cells snapped-off from around your endometrium,
embedding tiny splinters inside.

Your babies' never-feet are like your own:
in sands no one could pass through
without damage. If you choose to stand now

you choose to make wounds you could touch.
You're young and childless. Consider it:
outside this room there is nothing like you.

Escape

Out of the skin blur of my inner eyelids
his fag ends sweat into little fish.
Under this sea his exceeding wake
follows my family, and I –

Opening my eyes he is in the corner
with the same crooked nose as Mr. Punch.
I press my shadow face into his,
he would not hurt his friend.

But darkness smokes in weedy tendrils
under the bedroom door
like any minute it will learn
how to turn the door out.

Sometimes, he stands in front of me
in shops and streets, never turns round.
If I turn my back on him,
his face will turn on me.

Morrison's Box, first lockdown (after no food shopping for three weeks)

A cucumber! A cucumber!
The first yippee of the box. The only vegetable my oldest always eats

Carrots – vitamin a. Everyone will eat them. But not too many.

Cabbage – something just for us

More onions – we have so many onions. We are going to be ok

Potatoes – I had reserved two for you for your birthday but they're growing eyes. Now we will all have mummy's chips

Kitchen towel – I only buy it for birthdays and Christmas and this is like that.

Bog roll – Branded, nonetheless. I thought the kitchen towel might have been a stand in, to throw in the bin by the loo (not down the drain)

Tomato soup. Vegetable soup. Pasta stir in (I am so tired of thinking of every meal I am so relieved)

An insulation blanket. Tape. Ice packs

Mince – we haven't had beef since the UN gave us 12 years to save the planet with our weekly shop

Chicken breasts – protein

Ham. You wanted ham, little one!

Sausages! Bacon! Holiday breakfast!

Sunshine. Little one claims the scratchy insulation blanket as a comforter. I soothe my back with ice packs

Butter. Birthday cake is saved. (Who minds a little salt?)

Bread. Basic. Perfect

Cravendale. Is that milk?

Tracing Home in the Old Country

I have an address on a napkin. My brother
has the name of a church. I am surprised
he can remember anything, has agreed to the trip,
wants any shared reality with me. He wants no

shared reality with me. He is frightened by my
hand gestures as I drink coffee in what I dream
is the tearoom where our great-grandmother
took tea: she was the one who sent menus

to intimidate our widowed granny. My brother sees
things in my hands that I do not mean and would never
mean and I wish I could spell I love you and if
I could control your mind I would fix it you idiot. I

can't. The sky is pink and the hills are grey
and there is a rainbow of dark blues, pinks
and greens where they meet that I would dress
everyone in if I had a wedding or a ballet. There

is nothing where the family home is supposed
to be according to my napkin. There are homes
either side but the old residence is gone.
There is a space that would fit a house.

Things are growing wild there. Our name
is in the churchyard. In the pub loo, distracted,
I spill my Mooncup. My blood lines
the floor where we may or may not have been.

Sky Blue Pink

It's Hong Kong.
1957.
1952.
Are you there?

The sky — so you say —
is sky blue pink;

you have been showing me
since 1981.
Since 1983.

That blue with pink shot through
that happens in London Spring.
That happens in your silk portraits.
In the Hong Kong childhood
you tell and tell and tell.

It's London.
Are you there?
The sky is blue with pink edged clouds.
Does this count?

Three pigeons for yes.
A cloud shaped like a teddy bear
for no.

The sun cracking through for
you're there.

First Sight of Real Seals

Their heads out, curved eyes on us,
reciprocating the salty, convex cabin.
Look, there, beautiful wooden bowling balls,
said my mum. Then, *My contact lens is stuck,*
it had worked itself into her eyelid
and was cutting an imprint for a new eyeball.

I rescued her lens. We got into the smaller boat,
rowed to see Low Island, where one determined
wave had engorged a whole community
of monks, along with the island's centre.
In the deep slit seals blinked as I looked
at my hands, which hadn't flinched.

Wreck, Basement Flat, W11

The outskirts of my bunk were a lawn of seaweed,
through which I boated with my pirate crew:
a dozen seals, paired by name, like Thunder and Storm.
My bedroom blind was crooked (I'd tugged at it,
to seal it, too often) and it became a taut sail, in the wind –

which changed, made our sail flap, stopped our ship.
Everything was flat calm. I looked to my crew. Their eyes
were all to me, but they'd become fibrous and plastic.
They could not see me. I was alone. Strangers could see in.
Traffic passed
            and the window groaned like a hull about to split.

I dived out of bed, rushed through the hall, slowed
at the doorway of my mum's room. She was still awake too,
playing the piano a note at a time, her back to her bedroom door.
I stood a while in my own, new loneliness, then said
                                        BAH!

Mum sprang and fell back, from her wonky old piano stool
to her bed. Her arms still poised, hands clawed, legs bent,
still as an upturned bug. She waggled her legs. The broken
loud pedal, always down, left the notes she'd been playing
heaving out: a drone, uniting giggles and shrieks, swelling
the whole room into a hug, the groaning windows snuggling in.

Afterlife

I have found something for you to do, body,
when you've stopped carrying me. Your
loyal if short-lived service has moved me
in so many ways. I didn't want to leave

you with limited options; you've
behaved so differently to others' bodies. I
honour that. I've written to the faculty
and they've accepted you for a new role.

You will work with the students, opening
out the secrets of how you and I lasted together
as long as we did, in the circumstances.
The lines you've rewritten with blood and bile,

the prose-purple of our shared organs,
notches etched on the heart, will act
as a text-book love-letter to the future.
Body, know that I'm sad to leave.

University Dental Hospital, Tower Wing
(Fractured Crown Sequence)

He rubs his knuckle against my gum firmly,
as he, Raj, feels my teeth. We have long since
abandoned speech. He fixes a thread between
my bones. *Lower right six* catches in purple
rubber. He fits it into a yellowed, U-bent
lip. His eyes an inch from my purple smile,
his focus is unparalleled by any lover I've known.
For three hours, he keeps his face by mine, till he fits
four spikes more than an inch into my jaw and sends
me away to radiography. The wet that's swelled
behind the purple rubberdam drips on my sweater.
Raj has kept my dam in its clamp. I am to have
a plastic lollipop scratch the inside of my cheek
while I bite down on the smile he gave me.

While I bite down on the smile he gave me
Raj's smile is protected by a surgical mask.
He tells me not to forget he'll call,
make sure I am recovering, but I cannot
have his number. I believe him. I trust him
from the patience of his eyes on my mouth.
He gives me a form to prove I was here, consented
to leave his care, be referred to endo on Floor 25.
I can't look at his eyes now I'm standing up;
I look for my coat and my own plastic glasses.
As I go, a man is waiting by the x-ray room.
I see his purple rubberdam has been unclasped,
and it drools as a filigree tongue, so delicate, but
he is unsmiling, and turns away from me.

He is unsmiling, and turns away from me –
then this endodontist says, 'I've heard all about your teeth,
let me in,' like the wolf has put on Red Riding Hood's gown
and crept up behind my new chair. His eyes
inside the dental loupe are so big and close
and yet hidden; a wolf who's stuck dad's binoculars
onto granny's glasses. He pushes in his hands
as if in prayer, and then huffs, and puffs out my sense
of being safe in my reclining chair. Now
he is picking up his pen, he is taking my photograph
down, he leaves, his apprentice is levering me out,
handing me an empty discharge form. 'Extract it, then,
please,' I say, 'I won't find another dentist.'
'I wish I could help, but we follow his commands.' He bows.

'I wish I could help, but we follow his commands.' 'He' bows,
this stubborn Lower Left Seven, under Ellen's weight,
the tooth that Raj and then the wolf couldn't restore,
that nearly lost me a place in this tower before
I discovered Acute Day Care on Floor 23.
Ellen and her guide have plied and twisted him; now
he lets out his roots into the envelope Ellen has cut
and folded in my gum. What message has festered in his canals?
It cracks, creaks, leaks, bleeds, escapes
aspiration and writes itself over my chin,
rushes into my throat. I was hoping for a simple extraction
but a source has been opened and exposed, while I
am unable to see, taste, express and, barely, to move.
Ellen brushes my forehead, holds up a mirror.

Ellen brushes my forehead, holds up a mirror
to the roof of my mouth, while I watch the sky
outside the tower soften and shrink a little.
'Is that your eyes watering?' she says, looking
at them. 'It won't be too long now, stay brave.'
She is sharp and bright as the acuity of pain
in my hard-as-teeth gums when the anaesthetic went in.
'Your philtrum is quivering.' I close my eyes,
and hear song: *3,4,5,6 and there, there*
is caries in the abutment, amalgam in the distal molar.
The apex was deep, but the alveolus yields;
your cementum was like a seal, your mandible will hurt
but we've cared for you, cured you intraorally,
the mystery now is in the interproximal space.

The mystery now is in the interproximal space,
in whether the psychic realities in the waiting-room
daytime movie prove to be true, or the father
(the eminent psychiatrist who has taken his teenage
son and his sparky nine-year-old little sister
on holiday to an ancient lake with a sea monster)
is actually psychotic; the elderly Native American
thinks not, so I'm hopeful. Love prevails. The baddies dumping
toxic waste are exposed and extracted. Lightning
strikes like a needle and the bleeding skin on the monster
is finally relieved; the tunnel to its den clots.
I forgive the endodontist, say to the prosthodontist:
See you on some occlusal plane, on the imaginary
surface on which upper and lower teeth meet.

'Surface on which upper and lower teeth meet
compromised by bruxism. I wonder if there are
other things affecting your throat and wellbeing.
Are you stressed? You do clench and grind your teeth?
You need to start looking after yourself. We can help
with the cavities and the gingival hypertrophy you've earned
through poor self care, once your gum has healed up.
You will be returning for a bridge, or perio splints.'
I am thinking of the time the clamp got stuck
between lower right cuspid and bicuspid.
I'd had no anaesthetic, as there was no gingival contact
intended. Raj kept gripping, and trying to free it,
until his teacher widened the interproximal space.
I remember crying. I will be returning for a bridge.

Looking at Her Missing Brother's Paintings: 'Self Portrait as Child'

Your hair, the blond feathers that used to make me hug you
while you stood like a fork,
when we were in the years
I slept under the roof of your top bunk.

And the gutters of shadows, like a dark church. I used to
have a recurring nightmare that stayed in my waking.
In our local tube station, there was a swamp in place of tracks.
A row of pews made for a platform.
One night, it ended.
When I ran away from the pews, they were empty,
but I looked back and you were in them.
Your hair catching light from the thing advancing.

Soon after, you fell asleep on a bus in your own
private row
near the back, away from me. At the terminus,
I got off, met Dad
    and the bus drove away with you.
Dad called, I shrieked, you ran and hurled yourself
to the street.
Brother. Why do you still
stay later than the adventure, with too-bold innocence?

I will propose on Halloween

It is our Anniversary.
Slither in through the top window
of the bedroom, wrapped as a bat,
squeak out a ring with a hiss
and tiny teeth. Or doll up
in a feather bikini and coconut breasts,
with a taste for flesh, produce
the suggestion of engagement
from inside a nest of ringlets.
I haven't quite decided yet.
One thing is certain.
We will marry in a carnival,
a Mexican day of the dead,
friends and family dressed up
for a little warm death.

Shared Grief and the Orange of a Streetlamp

Each segment of the streetlamp's polygon's full as a satsuma. We need this lamp. Leaves in front are black. Behind, leaves and branches peel off dark as they move into the glow. Leaves under are fiery. Above, a halo. Then my window, bed, me.

Suddenly, the streetlamp dims. It doesn't go out. It's an orange philtrum, a mouth clasping unextinguishedness. Why is it so little lit? If we could we'd see the tree's less grey — daylight is rising. We look at nothing but the slightened lamp. In my bed I am held by this orange filament.

Now the lamp is not lit. It's a clear polygon, green-cased. The tree's green, wavering leaves obscure the lamp post. There's a dusting of grey still on the morning. It hurt our hearts when the orange glow went out. I am in bed. The other side of the window, there's just enough light now.

Under

Looking up at my impractical globe lampshade
(it gave my study a blue tinge), I noticed that
from my desk chair I saw only the Pacific, low
island countries. Atolls. Strange, I thought, to sit under
places scientists had us believe would go underwater.
Voyeur, I pictured our basement flat, near the Thames, flooding.
How it might, if it rained like it had been again; I carried
on working for as long as I could, till I had to go *xixi*,
and found a wet Elastoplast on the bathroom floor. I just
threw it into the sink, but later, I realised plasters, pills,
bandages were all soaked. The basin had been fitted with
a bath tap and had been leaking into a secret flood. Water
was streaming along the low bathroom shelf, into the wall,
under the floor. Now, my first aid kit is useless.

Sleep

My hair, in the sea, on the pillow
like home when I could share a room
tucked in bed near my bro

after making waves and soapy
Mohicans in the bath,
my hair now tugs and floats

towards tide-stream baldnesses
in mum's hair, a bruise-blue expanse,
hulks of broken bones.

The fear learned by my adult body
follows me to bed
and tosses my hair about.

The strands are lines to throw
to carry memories from before
like bathwater from tip to scalp.

To Sorrow

I felt you poke between my shoulder
blades once, Sorrow. I winced, first,
expecting a blow, then wondered how
a trailing shadow like you could
take on such body. With this thought
I turned you into a ghost, in my wake.

So, I bent my elbows back as I walked,
to keep you off. *Don't be unawares*,
I told myself, and chose to let you ride
with your hands gripping my
backward arms, to stop you breaking
onto me with a wave of blood and tears.

My back hurts from carrying the weight
of you like that and the tendon you
once poked from sprite height is still sore.

I'm forced to let my elbows drop.
You swing in front, like a monkey or
a papoose. I hold you out, arms' length;
you're a short, swaddled mass of spirit,
all torn and terror. You have been
skating on my skirts, arms up
to get my attention. Come here,
little thing, and stop your crying.

Looking at Her Missing Brother's Paintings: 'East Finchley Cemetery'

You can paint layers of darkness till the dark takes on shapes,
                                                              insists
it's full of light. I see something in what you've shaded between
                                                             tree boughs
and ground. An elliptical teardrop. Blurred, dusky outline made
                                                          by the scoop
of that dropping branch, the cup of that one, the slope of wood
                                                                  chips.

It's almost exactly what I want to show you, in negative. It's
                                                          where out-loud
words go, in pictures. My rib bones shade the same shape, over
                                                           and again.
I am racked with x-rays of ready speech bubbles.

     As I look longer,
dear, lost friend of a lifetime, I see it's a space, that you've filled
with barely-visible people. I am a flat-out bulge with a flick of
                                                                 toes.

My body is the speech bubble, bones and the spaces they shade
are open mouths drawn in. I am sure because, as I look, alone
                                                               here,
I feel myself lying in the chipping, in the distended bulb of
                                                                shadows.
My throat constricts, to seal me into the shape. I hear my bones
                                                                    cry.

Komodo Dragon

I met you on my way out of the forest,
big Komodo. Your moves so
like my mother's disease. I fell in step,
childhood myth, with your feet

up to that certain meet. You and me.
Details hazy. Your tail, smooth and thick,
on my cheek. You bit
then watched. I tried to look

at other possibilities. Birds
I hadn't seen before, a snake
in the distance. Wild boar running off
into the sunset, their gleeful legs.

I came to and saw you watching me,
crocodile eyes. I picked up
with a rickshaw driver. Pedalling muscles
twitched solid as your tail.

He woke with punctured tyres.
I walked to the airport. Knew you
were in the overhead luggage bins.
I now continue with things

as if you've gone. But I've been
foraging, reading, eating berries,
standing against the open fire.
I know I must be close

and hope the rustle in the bush,
skins in the bathtub, two glimmers
in the corner of my bedroom,
prove to be you, waiting for me.

**My Garden Explains Endometriosis and Laparoscopy
(When I Can't)**

Her hormones are my weeds. As her garden, I am growing
like her illness. Up close to me, you'll find thorns and roots
twisting under my surface, as if you could tug and see
the whole lawn tear. Creeping cinquefoil has implanted itself

in the wrong places. Its leaves imitate hemp, the way rogue
cells mimic her womb's lining. Bindweed's white adhesions
thread her insides and mine. Bramble-angry reds sound alarm:
soon nothing will be fertile, soon everything scarred and choked.

A gardener wearing the label 'medicus' puts hands in our beds
and says: *Now we've cleared the soil, the time to plant*

is uncertain, but certainly limited. She is in recovery too.
Diathermy has cleared her like propane weed burners.
She sleeps half-raised, her abdomen sometimes flowering a rose.

As she heals from within her womb, so I take time with compost.
She takes her legs, touches sepal-thick hairs, speaks at last, says,
Look, my love, if I brush my skin a thousand seeds lie sparkling on me.

Halfway Home

Three months after we escaped
from tides of violence in our home,
remember that we stopped
the car near Barley Cove
and headed with our lunch
for the biggest, smoothest stone.

Closer we saw it was my childhood
bedfriend, a grey seal, marooned.
We both crept round to the front.
The seal had no eyes, only blood.
We drove back to our borrowed refuge,
but damp walls had wept the sheets through.

Army of Teeth
After Cadmus and the Dragon's Teeth

Although my lips and tongue dissolve,
although my mouth grows darker,
although my fire is out, my teeth
in all their crowned, filled glory
spring up through the soil, shoot out, and walk.

Upper Right Five — porcelain and alloy,
after pregnancy decay and a baby's headbutt —
strides in her crown between living rooms
and pillow-plumped beds, brings
china cups of tea to feeding mums.

Cracked and pressured Lower Right Seven,
so long alone at the back by uprooted Six,
years of taking all the weight,
nearly full of composite amalgam, soars
in her tin rocket, to the moon.

Upper Left One, resin resilient,
moves mercury-quick between women
and those men who would destroy them.
Canals are filled with my little silver warriors,
who give passage, slay werewolves.

The cries of my army of teeth
can be heard from the moon to the home.
Ground down Upper Left Five,
she stays, strokes my bare-bone forehead,
combs my copper hair into verdigris roots.

Lines

The seal lying across the crest of the waves like a log
pesters the line between life and death.

We get into the car. The log-like bulk disappears.
Mum and I return to the stony beach, to wait,

I say, *For it to come back up. Its position was strange.*
Usually it's just heads, round as ball-point pen bases.

I suspect we have both decided it's dead, and add,
breathless, *or like pen-seals.* My mum stares

till the seal reappears, paddling, playing.
'You panicked, Toad, and fell off a log,'

she shouts. On the horizon
the Fast Net lighthouse is lit by the sun.

Loss

The only way I could say it
would be to get in with the sea,
learn the expression it makes
as it hits the rocks and breaks.

Safety at Sea

A seal pup is a raindrop on a toenail
from here – where Mum and I cross at Mizen Head
the bridge between cliffs, to the last land
before the Fastnet lighthouse, to the small,
white museum of Safety at Sea. The seal
pup is a blob on a rock in the gulf.

I need lenses, but this is a pup, its grey-white
writhing, the strain of its pulpy neck
in its never-finished mewl, that mouth,
and the placidity of its tail in spite of itself.
Alone, on a rock in the choppy waves,
an unreachable island vision beyond it.

In the onlooking cliff face, there's a cut-out
shadow, shaped like a mother seal, whose image
does not recede with each increasing wave.

Does it Snow at Sea?

Yes, at the edge I watch it land
It sits a few inches deep
Coagulates the surface
Stiffens almost, stilling.

Closer, snow-covered rocks
shale into the water and clear
Show light underneath
The sea is not a grey, blanket shroud

over nothing.

See that thick line, how it ripples?
Fish, swimming about, shoaling.

And the other side, the moon
rises like an aura
through the snow fog.

On Watching a Cob and Pen Kissing on the Serpentine at Sunset

Two swans necking makes a single heart
which frames lake and sunset in its hollow
so the old, corny love - two into one -
makes a nothing of what's natural.

Also, someone once told me
if you put a swan in a poem
it gets violent.

The pen dips her head,
nibbles her mate to groom
and I'd rather pen something
about my corn on your cob.

First

Becoming still, in the oblong
of light across the bed,
he asks what we should call us.
He and I both close our eyes
on the question. Half-sleeping,

I see a shelf in Oxfam,
Ken High Street, 1982,
as my mum lifts me to where
my opal, burbling dreams take form
with the first touch of softness.

'What is?' I ask. 'Seal,'
she says, taking it to the counter.
The shop carpet is shallow,
makes my teeth hurt a little,
is no place for my hands.

The paving rolls the buggy along,
we mow bogey fingers in the cracks.
Splots of rain flatten the seal's fur;
I curl my body out and over it.
The pavement slows.

Mum's face noses mine.
'What is its name?'
There's only one answer
in the language I have, 'Seal.'
She pulls the plastic cover over us both.

Rain plays on the bedroom skylight.
The back of my hand is on his chest,
the coarse, black hairs there still wet.
My fingers are in the air between us,
palms full of what his skin breathes out.

The Intense Synaesthesia of Belonging

Here in the Barbican tonight, the orchestra wear
lace and comfortable bodies.
My body is all their instruments.
The double bass, my tummy.
The timpani is my sternum:
home, home, let me go home let me go home.

And now I am rolling about the long-gone
floor of the corridor in my old home
till I know how it tastes, chanting:
Every bee has its own hum.
If I am someone else's dream
I hope I am a good one.

Violin bows are pins in the living room carpet.
Granny Evie is on the sofa, in a good mood.
You see, it was the earnest,
lamest little things
little percussions of minor chaos
that she enjoyed.

Granny Evie: now you're here too
I have a question for you.
When concerts are put on the radio,
why do they clap for *so long*?
Who wants to listen to clapping
on the radio? Granny Evie leaves.

The orchestra pass the note between
such different size instruments
like love, parent to child.
Some is written, some impro.
Now my cat is on my piano
walking up and down.

Musicians with their strings and bows,
me with my old room full of toys,
books, pens and paper.
We are so responsible
for the meaning
of inanimate things.

I long for rain like I used to,
listening to the music,
see mud, moon.
Maybe you are the little life inside
lit by the piano
that needs to be loved.

> *You will see*
> *the golden glow*
> *as well as the shadow*
> *when you look again*
> *at the orchestra*
> *still playing.*

Reading the Sea

The whalewatcher proves there's a path to the sun.
On that weightless gold way across the sea

he shows us taut footprints, plumped with whale memory,
their edges seamed with beads.

One of the parents calls, *Something in the water*:
not a whale now but a seal, tummy down.

Flapping each side of the back of his head is a beardy Grecian
                                                                                            coil:
the seal's face, split and opened out by the ocean.

The children see its edges crumbling like sponge in spilt
                                                                        lemonade,
parents, the moss-ish curls that float in derelict places.

I see cake dropped in the bath, and the children, quiet, looking
over the edge, into the waves. All swell, all swell, all swell.

Indigo Dreams Publishing Ltd
24, Forest Houses
Cookworthy Moor
Halwill
Beaworthy
Devon
EX21 5UU
www.indigodreamspublishing.com